DAVID BOOTH / ALMUTH BARTL

Everybody Wins

Games for Active Learning in K-6 Classrooms

Illustrations: Dorothee Wolters

Pembroke Publishers Limited

Pembroke Publishers
538 Hood Road
Markham, Ontario, Canada L3R 3K9
www.pembrokepublishers.com

Distributed in the U.S. by Stenhouse Publishers
477 Congress Street
Portland, ME 04101
www.stenhouse.com

Fun-Olympics Sport © 1999 Verlag an der Ruhr, Alexanderstrasse 54, 45472
Muelheim/Ruhr, Germany

Everybody Wins © 2000 Pembroke Publishers

Canadian Cataloguing in Publication Data

Booth, David
    Everybody wins : games for active learning in K–6 classrooms

Includes bibliographical references and index.
ISBN 1-55138-123-0

1. Educational games. 2. Group work in education. 3. Education, Primary – Activity
programs. I. Bartl, Almuth. II. Title.

LB1029.G3B65 2000   372.133'7   C00-931557-8

Editors: Cynthia Young, Deborah Sherman
Cover Design: John Zehethofer
Cover Illustration: Dorothee Wolters
Typesetting: JayTee Graphics

Printed and bound in Canada
9 8 7 6 5 4 3 2 1

Contents

Introduction

Learning through Playing

Human beings tend to be good learners. Our brains and "human intellect" allow us to receive, organize, synthesize, integrate, and apply an enormous amount of diverse information. This is especially true when we are children.

In every culture around the world, children achieve significant learning through playing games, whether they are on-the-spot role-plays or structured games with specific rules. Playing games provides opportunities for children to acquire information, hone physical skills, interact with others, explore new interests, discover new abilities, and try out adult roles.

Joining In

By their very nature, games encourage us to "join in," "participate," "be part of this human experience." Games let us celebrate being together. No matter our size, our age, or our ability, we are welcome inside the ring. By joining in with others, we are part of a larger whole. The activities and games in this book will help children join in, meet others, wake up the body, release the energy in the room, and encourage the spirit of play that is at the heart of playing games.

Playful interaction builds its own momentum, quickly catching the spirit, energy, and excitement inherent in learning through games. But first, each child must take that initial risk of "joining in." Each activity encourages participation in a non-threatening and positive manner, nudging children into *wanting* to be a part of the action. In the early stages of group development, the students' attempts at joining in must be supported by the leader and other group members. As the leader of the game, you have an opportunity to teach and demonstrate that the fun comes from the experience of playing, not from winning. This means that at first, competition should be minimal or non-existent. Players should not be excluded or shut out but, instead, should be *brought back into* the game quickly. As leader, you must find ways to help the players participate for the sake of the game and promote the fellowship that arises from taking part in the same activity that others are doing.

Games are not haphazard inventions, but rather, social structures that allow the players to learn without making them feel they have to. The games and activities in *Everybody Wins* present clear tasks and objectives, but it is the process of achieving them that holds the learning.

Building Cooperation

Everybody Wins offers a variety of games and activities that you can use for active, hands-on learning in different settings and for diverse purposes. In these games, the children will constantly evaluate their own actions and those of other players, learning to negotiate, yield, and compromise. At first, their actions may be simply rule-driven; however, as they recognize the consequences of their decisions, the children can begin to consider other options. Games allow the players to be aware of group dynamics in action — learning by doing. Of equal value, games offer players the chance to use these experiences and processes in new contexts in the future.

Games are about challenge, but challenge doesn't have to mean individual competition. The tension and excitement in a game can just as easily arise from the players' need to cooperate while they search together for a solution to the game's problem. As the group leader, you can be freed from the usual authoritative adult role

because the structure of the game develops a dynamic that will control the group's behavior. The players themselves hold the power to bring fun and satisfaction to the game. Games and group activities have a natural dynamic that controls the group's behavior. As soon as the players know the rules and how a game works, they can take charge of the playing. The games and activities in *Everybody Wins* truly belong to the youngsters.

Everyone Is a Winner!

Everyone is a winner when they participate in an activity or a game, whether they are a single player, a team member, a referee, or a timekeeper, and whether they are playing to test or improve their own achievement, or to measure their knowledge or skill in competition with others.

Encourage students to share this winning attitude by recognizing the efforts and contributions of all participants. Recognition is easy: *Everyone* who takes part receives some kind of award or souvenir. (For example, students on the first aid committee and parents or other volunteers who come in to help with scoring and refereeing should receive an award or souvenir for their contribution to the event.)

On Your Mark...

Getting Ready for the Games

Games can be played anywhere, anytime, and they do more than just enhance the learning. Games can supply the medium for growth, help to calm excited children, increase energy, focus energy, release tension, and develop sensitivity and awareness. When children work together, they magnify the fun at the same time that they develop and refine new skills and knowledge. The games and activities in *Everybody Wins* offer versatility. You can use several at one time for game days, field days, first and last day of school celebrations, theme days, integrated arts festivals, cooperative learning, peer coaching, team building, camps and recreation centres, or a single game during a lesson about one specific topic.

- Whenever you attend athletic events or live performances/ entertainment, take notes about all positive and negative aspects you experienced. Moreover, you might get to know about fascinating citizens of your town who might enrich your *Everybody Wins* event, for example, a juggling nurse or a roller-blading mayor.

If a famous athlete lives in your city, ask this person to offer special training in his or her area of expertise. Student sports enthusiasts will find this very exciting. As well, you can get some autographs from the athlete and use them as prizes.

Many students will be familiar with the Summer and Winter International Olympic Games held every four years. Children are frequently captivated by the pageantry and excitement of the Olympic Games — the colorful parades, different flags, awards ceremonies, as well as the competitive nature of the athletic events. You can increase student interest and participation in your own activities, games, and challenges by building on their knowledge of and natural attraction to events such as the Olympic Games.

The *Everybody Wins* Flag

Get the children involved right at the start by inviting them to design and create their own special *Everybody Wins* flag. Hang the flag in a spot that is clearly visible to all the children. Let them know that when they see the flag, they can expect a special learning experience. See the activity "Making an *Everybody Wins* flag, on page 22.

Awards, Medals, and Souvenirs

Awards, medals, and souvenirs will keep the memory and spirit of a special activity or event alive. Whenever possible, have students actively involved in making the awards, medals, and souvenirs. This provides an important area in which several children can contribute to the group effort and overall enjoyment. Be sure to have some special form of

recognition for these children, too. You will find instructions for making awards on page 23.

Awards can be as simple as a small foil-wrapped treat, or as elaborate as a bronze, silver, or gold medal with a ribbon that identifies individuals by name. Consider using different kinds of awards at different times. For example, for a Field Day, Games Day, or School Olympics event, you might choose to have more elaborate medals, while small treats might be more appropriate if you are using a single activity to teach a specific concept in a core subject.

Other forms of recognition include a videotape of the event, a mention in the student newspaper, signing a special events autograph book, or being in a team photo exhibited in the school foyer. Parent volunteers and/or children who are not involved in a specific event can be asked to be reporters, photographers, and videographers. A scrapbook of articles, photographs, and autographs from the games can be kept as a class or school record. The scrapbook can be displayed at the school's open house or parent-teacher meetings.

Awards, Medals, and Souvenirs for Special Circumstances

Pre-game excitement can lead to disappointment if a child becomes ill or is unable to attend/participate in the games. A kind gesture is to send an honorary award or souvenir to the unfortunate student who cannot take part. These mementos could include photos of the student's team with a note and their signatures, or perhaps an honorary medal if their team won a gold, silver, or bronze.

Get Set...

Decorations for a Large Event

The following items are all part of the decorations for a large event: the *Everybody Wins* flag, a winners' platform with a red carpet, balloons in the *Everybody Wins* colors, a velvet cushion, a lost and found box, a drinks stand, and an information stand with speakers. It can be helpful to assign a group of three students to be responsible for keeping the decorations looking their best for the duration of the event.

event flag

balloons

flags of countries

drink stand

cushion

lost and found

winners' platform

information stand

Staying Power

Some people, especially teenagers, somehow disappear during the course of an event, and get involved in doing something else. However, there are some ways that can assist you in keeping students involved. You could hold a lottery with attractive prizes, perhaps a new CD, tickets to a local professional sports event, or tickets to a movie. Do not announce the winners until the final ceremonies. This can help to ensure that students don't wander off in the middle of the games.

A lost and found box is useful and can be maintained by the decoration team. Students, referees, and volunteers should bring all caps, socks, bags, etc. that have been found to the lost and found box. Anyone who discovers he or she has lost an item, should check there first. If there are still things left at the end of the event, they should be placed in the school's lost and found immediately.

Forming Groups and Teams

Although there are bound to be times when children want to be grouped with friends, such groupings may not be in the best interests of the activity or the learning. However, organizing groups and teams doesn't have to be difficult. Here are two possible ways to select players randomly.

Many games will require the same number of players for each team. To avoid quarrels among the players, draw lots to determine the teams. For example, say the game needs two teams with seven players. Cut seven strips of red cloth and seven strips of blue cloth and place them in a basket. Mix up the strips. Then, without looking, each player takes a strip of cloth, which can be worn as a headband or armband to distinguish the players on the teams.

Blindfold all the students. Play some music and let the students dance. Stop the music and call out, "Groups of three!" (or four, or five, etc.). The blindfolded students have to get together, thus forming their group or team.

The *Everybody Wins* Mascot

Some students may be familiar with the mascot of a favorite professional sports team. Explain to the children that the *Everybody Wins* mascot is a little bit different. The *Everybody Wins* mascot consists of as many children as possible.

The students line up one behind another and wait in a crawling position. The game leader then covers the children with a sheet or blanket. When everybody is covered by this "skin," and only the head of the first youngster can be seen, the mascot starts to move forward. To prevent the mascot from breaking up as it moves, the children must hold onto the ankles of the person crawling in front of them.

The mascot should try to travel to as many game and activity sites as possible, if you are holding a multiple-game event.

The *Everybody Wins* Cushion

Decorate an old duvet cover with the *Everybody Wins* symbols. Fill the sack completely with balloons. Athletes who are not active for a certain time can have a rest on this sack of balloons. This special *Everybody Wins* cushion can be used to carry some of the most successful athletes for their "lap of honor."

Timekeeping

The easiest way to keep the time is with a stopwatch. However, there are funnier and more entertaining "time-keeping instruments" that you can use. These other instruments have the advantage of allowing more children to be involved in a game or activity, without necessarily being an actual player.

- Estimate the length of time the game or activity should last. Have the children choose a song that runs about the same length of time.

While the teams play, the children sing the song. Play ends when the song is finished.

- Select an easy set of cooking instructions (such as those on a package of spaghetti). While the teams play, one student reads the recipe — backwards!

- Set a time limit based on the amount of time it takes for the other children to say the alphabet twenty times, or perhaps go through the times-tables from one through six.

Safety Station

The games and activities are intended to be fun; however, accidents and overexertion can occur. Consider setting up a Safety Station to deal with these kinds of problems. The following ideas may help you to set up a basic Safety Station:

- An emergency telephone should be available. The telephone numbers for the hospital, police, fire station, and dentist can be posted beside the telephone. It is also a good idea to have the numbers of all the parents, in case of an accident.

- Set up in a cool, shady area so that hot, tired, or injured students can rest and cool down.
- Have chairs and at least one cot and a sleeping bag or a blanket available.
- Keep a first aid kit at the Safety Station. If possible, have an adult first aid provider on duty.
- There is an activity called "Ambulance Team" (see page 63). It is actually designed to provide a brief *rest* for children who have been playing. Students who are on the Ambulance Team can set up at the Safety Station.

GO!

Opening Ceremonies

Introduce the games with the *Everybody Wins* Laws and the *Everybody Wins* Oath. Remind students that these laws and the oath are very special.

The *Everybody Wins* Laws

- You have to clap your hands three times before speaking.
- All students are to address boys as "Sir" and girls as "Lady."
- The following words are "taboo," for example "yes," "no," etc.

The *Everybody Wins* Oath

At the opening ceremonies, one of the players takes an oath for all participants. Give this student the flag to hold in his or her left hand. With the right hand raised, the student says the following oath: "In the name of all participants I hereby declare that we will respect the *Everybody Wins* rules and joyfully participate and honor all teams."

Warming Up

Students should warm up before they participate in physical activities. Every player gets a chance to be the leader in the following warm up.

Have all the children line up. When the referee blows the whistle, the first player starts running, and adds a quick exercise, such as running zigzag or doing a somersault. The other students must copy the first player's exercises. When the referee blows the whistle again, the first player goes to the back of the line. Now the second player starts to run, and adds a different exercise...and so on. When everyone has warmed up, the games can begin.

Breathers

No matter how much fun everyone is having, make sure that players have a chance to catch their breath. These two ideas can be used to help children rest and refocus before the next event.

- Passing the Time: All the children sit in a circle. Set a small alarm clock so that it will ring in one minute, and put the clock in a bag. Students pass the bag from one person to the next. The person holding the bag when the alarm clock rings, has to drop out. Keep resetting the clock and playing until there is only one person left.

- Tower Power: Obtain a large quantity of items that can be stacked to build a tower (e.g., building blocks, paper or plastic cups, tin cans). Organize the students into teams. Which team can build the highest tower within the time limit? (Give the teams two minutes.)

Thirst Quenchers

Participating in physical activities makes everyone thirsty. Students will enjoy the extra effort put into a drinks stand that provides special drinks. The following are good thirst quenchers:

- Apple Float: Mix 2 parts apple juice, 1 part sparkling mineral water. Add frozen grapes.
- Lemon Soda: Use a lemonade mix, and replace the water with sparkling mineral water.
- Ice Cube Juice: Use a variety of fruit juices of different colors to make ice cubes. Players can choose cubes in their favorite colors. Pour mineral water over the cubes.

The Closing Ceremonies

The end of large sports events usually includes special Closing Ceremonies. Here are some proposals to make your closing ceremonies special:

- Play "Medal Marbles." (See page 24 for instructions.)
- All athletes gather for a group picture. Smile!
- The organization team is honored by the children with medals.
- Conduct short live interviews with the outstanding athletes of the event.
- Everyone wins something, in teams or individually.
- The event organizer gives a short speech (three minutes or less) and officially declares the event to be ended.

Games
and
Activities

The *Everybody Wins* Flag

You will need an old sheet, two sticks or a clothesline, pushpins or clothes pegs, hot-glue gun, and materials for decorating the flag (e.g., wax crayons, felt-tipped markers, poster paints, scraps of fabric, buttons, embroidery thread, yarn).

Show the students flags for different countries, organizations, or teams. Conduct a short discussion about the purpose of a flag, and the use of symbols and logos. Use the school's flag as an example.

Now have the children design their own flag for the *Everybody Wins* games and activities. Arrange the students in groups of four. Give them ten minutes to brainstorm ideas for the flag. Each group shares their ideas with the rest of the class. The children can vote for their favorite ideas. Each group is responsible for doing a specific part of the flag.

Find a prominent place to put the flag. Use the clothes pegs to hang the finished flag on the clothesline, or attach it to the two sticks with the pins.

Geography — flags are a good way to identify different countries. Show students flags from various countries and ask them to locate the country on a world map.

Art — encourage students to think about the aesthetics of the colors, material combinations, and spatial arrangements. Introduce the idea that an artist sometimes visualizes a design before beginning a project.

Making Awards, Medals, and Souvenirs

You will need cardboard drink coasters, gold-, silver-, copper-toned metal foil, colored paper, ribbon, glue, and scissors.

Ask students what they know about medals and awards for sports events. Many sports competitions provide a special award to the winning team (e.g., Stanley Cup for NHL hockey) or individual awards for the top three athletes (e.g., gold, silver, and bronze medals for the world championships of skating).

Organize the students into groups of three or four. All the students can make the same style of award, or you can let each group design and make a series of different ones. If you want students to make a standard design, use the following as a guideline:

- Cut and glue the foil or paper onto the cardboard drink coasters.
- Each student cuts one strip of ribbon that can be loosely tied around their neck. They should fold the ribbon in half, making a "V" shape. The children can then glue the pointed end of the "V" to the back of the coaster, and tie it around their neck.

As an alternative approach, the following idea can be fun. Students enhance the medals with a "surprise" written on the back of the coaster. Surprises might be one of the following:

- The other winners will carry you for one "lap of honor" around the stadium.
- You are allowed to have a seat in the spectators' area, and you may watch the next game as a guest of honor.
- Choose your favorite song and all the athletes will sing it for you.
- This coupon entitles you to one Games Day, Field Day, or School Olympics photograph.
- Choose five athletes. Each one must tell a joke.
- You may choose the next game to be played, and all athletes have to take part.

Art — encourage students to think about the aesthetics of the medals, awards, and souvenirs.

Medal Marbles

You will need ten marbles, one cushion, extra medals, awards, souvenirs, and tape or chalk.

Place a medal on the cushion, which has been put in the middle of a large empty area (e.g., playground). Mark a starting line with chalk or tape. In groups of ten, students roll a marble from the starting line towards the pillow. The student whose marble is closest to the medal on the pillow wins it. (**Note:** This is a good game to play when you have extra medals left after the games.)

Math — students estimate and measure the distance to the pillow.

Science — discuss how surfaces can change the speed and direction of a moving object.

"Peanut" Tennis

You will need Styrofoam "peanuts" in a large box or bowl, four brand new fly swatters, chalk or tape for the starting line, and four buckets of sand.

Mark a starting line and place the buckets of sand 3 metres (10 feet) from the line.

Give each tennis player a fly swatter to use as a tennis racket. The players stand behind the starting line. Let each player pick up one Styrofoam "peanut" to start with. When the referee says "Go!" players try to hit the "peanuts" into their bucket of sand. After three minutes, the person who gets the most "peanuts" into their bucket wins.

(Of course, "peanut" tennis can also be played as doubles. In that case, two players work as a team to hit the most "peanuts" into the same bucket.)

Math — students estimate and measure the distance to the bucket.

Science — demonstrate force and motion and investigate the different properties of the Styrofoam peanuts and the fly swatters.

25

The Knot Competition

You will need four chairs or a bench, and four pieces of cord 1 metre (3 feet) long. The players sit next to each other on chairs or on a bench. Place a cord on the ground in front of each student. As soon as a starting signal is given, the players try to tie a knot with their feet. The first person to succeed shouts, "Stop!" and wins the game. (**Note:** You may want to have younger players form simple shapes like triangles, hearts, fishes, instead of a knot. Older students can make shapes as well, as a geometry exercise.)

Physical Education — develops motor skills.

Math — incorporates geometry and spatial arrangements.

Language Arts — students explain in writing how they did this activity.

Wrestling in the Ring

You will need chalk and a large playing area. Students can help with this set-up. With chalk or tape, draw a circle with a 1.5 metre (5 feet) diameter on the playground. Two children sit down back-to-back in the circle. After the starting signal, the two players try to press each other out of the circle. The spectators can cheer for their favorite players. However, make sure that there are fans for both players! After all the players have wrestled, the winners go on wrestling against each other, until there are only three winners left.

Social Studies/History — the competitive aspect of this game, with each side having a cheering section, makes an interesting introduction to feuding countries. Discuss countries or people at war or in dispute with each other over an issue.

Single Football

You will need a sandpit or grassy area and several table tennis balls. Mark or ask a student helper to mark the starting line along one edge of the area.

The object of the game is for players to throw a ball as far as possible. But not with their hands — with their feet. Players sit at the edge of the marked area, holding a table tennis ball with their feet. They throw the ball from the starting line, and their results are marked and measured by the linesperson.

Language Arts — introduce the concept of the element of surprise in stories. The children should recognize that the concept was used in this activity when they learned they would use their feet, not their hands, to throw the ball.

Throwing High

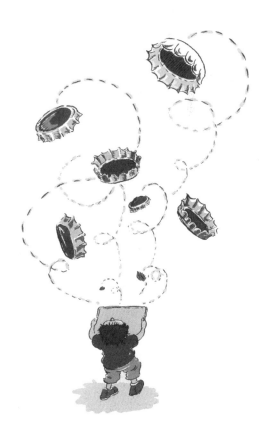

You will need ten "crown" bottle caps arranged on a tray.

In turn, students throw the bottle caps into the air by pushing the tray upwards, over their heads. Each cap that lands in its original position, and not upside down, counts for one point. When all students have had their turn, the person with the highest score is the winner.

An alternative procedure is to place the bottle caps on the floor. Standing about 3 metres (10 feet) away, the players try to hit the caps with tennis balls to make them jump and land right side up.

Science/Math — tie this game to a lesson about chance or probability. Relate probability to the repetition of experiments. Scientific investigations usually include a large number of test subjects. The actual experimental tests are repeated over and over by other scientists to confirm the findings.

Throwing Down

You will need three small stones for each player, and a plastic bottle. You must be able to tell the students' stones apart, so they should be marked differently. You will also need a platform of some kind (e.g., a low table or ledge) that students can stand on.

Place the bottle about one metre (3 feet) away from the platform. Three players at a time attempt to throw their stones directly into the bottle.

This is not very easy; therefore, give everybody a trial run before the game starts.

The most skilful throwers keep playing against each other until three winners are left.

Science — explore how distance affects accuracy. Move the bottle closer and farther away, and ask students to predict the results, and then test their ideas.

Frisbee

You will need nine paper cups and a stack of thick paper plates. Set up the nine cups like pins for bowling.

Give each player a paper plate. Each student throws a plate, attempting to hit as many cups as possible. The top-scoring players play each other, and the game continues until there are only three winners left.

Language Arts — compare the paper plate to a spaceship. What do the students think about space travel? Ask them to write a story or a report about their ideas.

Science — this activity can begin a lesson about the principles of flight. Why did the paper plate stay in the air? Why did it fall to the ground? What properties does it have that helps it or hinders it?

Javelin Throwing

You will need a javelin for each player, a hoop or a wire ring, and tape for the starting line. The javelins can be made from a measuring stick, a paint brush, or an empty paper-towel roll. (Use the same kind of item for each player's javelin, but put a mark on them so they can be matched to the throwers.)

Attach the hoop or wire ring to the branch of a tree at approximately the students' shoulder height. Mark the starting line about 5 metres (16 feet) from the hoop. The players line up at a starting line to throw their javelins.

Javelins must go through the hoop to be valid. Players who miss the hoop may throw a second time. The place where the javelin touches the ground is marked with a stone. The winner is the person with the farthest throw.

Language Arts — encourage students to use their research skills. They can check out the Internet or library resources to find out which countries placed first, second, and third in the most recent Summer and Winter Olympics.

Archery

You will need a blanket, a big ball or a box, and three little balls (e.g., table tennis balls or tennis balls). (**Note:** Use a larger ball or box to make it easier for students to score a hit. If you want to keep the box for future use, tape all the edges of the box.) Mark a starting line and place the blanket about 20 metres (65 feet) away from the line.

One of the players stands at the starting line and throws the big ball or box in a high arc towards the blanket on the floor. The other students throw the smaller balls and try to hit the box or ball while it flies through the air. This will be more difficult than the students expect; however, with a little practice it will become easier. Players get one point for hitting the box or large ball. After ten throws, the winner is the person who hits the box most often.

Discus Throwing

You will need a hat stand and a cap or other hat. Put the hat stand in the middle of the lawn or the playground.

Using the cap or hat as the discus, players throw it toward the hat stand. The goal is to have the hat land on the stand. Each child is allowed to throw three times, and all the hits are noted.

If the scores are tied, the best athletes have to throw again until three winners are left.

Guidance — a great activity for Careers Day. Have as many different "hats" as possible, and discuss the different occupations that each hat represents.

Table Tennis Without a Table

You will need chalk, string or cord, books or wooden boards. Mark out a "table" on the playground with a piece of chalk. Place a string or cord across the middle of the table. In case there are no table tennis rackets available, just use books or wooden boards instead.

The rules are the same as for regular table tennis.

Creative Thinking —this game is a "substitute" for "real" table tennis. Explain this concept to the students. Ask them to imagine that they are lost in a dense forest. They have food, but no shelter. Ask them to use their thinking skills to find a "substitute" for a tent.

Hockey

You will need a chair, an old umbrella, and a small ball (e.g., tennis ball). Place the chair in the middle of the lawn or playground, and mark a starting line approximately 20–30 metres (65-100 feet) away.

All the hockey players gather at the starting line. The first player turns the umbrella upside down and hits the ball to make it roll or fly between the chair legs. Players have three shots each time. Players who hit the ball through the chair legs at least once out of three times may have another turn. The game is played until only three winners are left.

Language Arts — introduce comparing two objects. Bring in a "real" hockey stick and the "umbrella" hockey stick and ask the children to describe how they are alike and how they are different.

Trampolining

You will need a table tennis ball and a garbage can that is opened by stepping on a pedal.

Place the table tennis ball on the lid of the can. (By the way, the most difficult part of this game is making the ball stay on the lid of the garbage can.) The athlete's task is to step strongly on the opening pedal, thus making the ball fly as far as possible. The referee marks down the achieved distance. Each athlete has three turns, and the person whose ball goes the longest distance is the winner.

Science — introduces the concept of balance and the centre of gravity.

Bottle Squirting

You will need 20 small paper cups, a waterproof pen or wax crayons, an empty squirtable plastic bottle (e.g., an empty liquid dish-soap bottle), a table, and a bucket of water for filling the bottle.

Write a number from 0–10 on the bottom of each paper cup. Then place the cups upright in random order on the table. Give each squirter exactly 30 seconds to knock over as many cups as possible. Add the numbers from the bottoms of the knocked over cups to determine the player's score. A medal is given to the person with the highest number of points. (**Note:** Students should note that both skill and luck are involved in winning this game.)

Math — instead of adding the scores on the cups, students multiply or divide the numbers for extra mathematics practice.

Careful Long Distance Running

You will need a bottle of soap. Mark a starting line and finish line.

Students line up behind the starting line. The first competitor takes the marked. The other players take their turns one by one. The person who transported their bubble the farthest is the winner.

bottle of soap and blows a soap bubble. The player must start to push and blow the bubble towards the finish line. When the bubble breaks the player has to stop, and the place is

Science — transporting soap bubbles is an excellent demonstration of structure and stability in science. Discuss why soap bubbles often have a rainbow and why they break so easily.

High Jump

You will need a wall and different colors of chalk.

The athletes line up at the wall. Each player gets a different color of chalk. The first player jumps as high as possible and uses the chalk to mark the highest point he or she can reach.

The other students follow suit. The referee can easily determine which player jumped the highest.

Social Studies — adapt this activity to introduce a social studies discussion: Is food distributed fairly around the world? Put your tallest students together on one team and the shortest students on the other team. Measure the height reached for each player, then total and average them. Students will quickly suggest that "it's not fair" because all the tall people were on one team!

Throwing the "Hammer"

You will need a large lawn or grassy area for this game.

Select a strong child to stand in the middle of the lawn at a safe distance from the spectators. A second child gives his or her hand to the first, who whirls and turns the second youngster around like a "hammer." After a while, the whirling comes to an end, and the strong child gently lets go of the other child. The next child in line is immediately pulled in to be used as a "hammer" — and the fun goes on.

Art — have each whirling child "freeze" and become a "statue." Other members of the class can use papier mache or modelling clay to make a statue of the child.

Weightlifting

You will need a class set of identical books (e.g., math books).

All the weightlifters line up leaving some space between players. Each athlete gets one copy of the book, which they lay flat on the palm of their hand. As soon as the starting signal is given, the students stretch out their arms. After a while, the arm with the book grows heavy and tired, and one weightlifter after another will give up until there are only three players left.

Science — examine the structure of the human body and its systems. Discuss why the book "becomes heavy" after a while.

Word Race

You will need a poster, paper, and pencils or pens for the players. Put the name of your school or a meaningful phrase on the poster in capital letters.

Give each player a piece of paper and a pen or pencil. Players have five minutes to form as many words as possible using the letters on the poster. The person who has written down the most words is the winner of the game.

All — apply this activity to terminology or vocabulary in any subject for a review.

The Statue

You need a sturdy raised platform, such as a desk.

This game does not aim at winning any medals, but guarantees a lot of fun. The children take turns climbing onto the platform and resting in various poses without moving. The chosen pose can correspond to any sport, or if you wish, to another topic that students are studying. Some sports poses that are easy to guess are rowing, boxing, fencing, and shot-putting.

Drama — instead of one student, have up to four students work together to make a tableau. The tableau should have an obvious meaning or story.

Snail Race

You will need a large object that can be decorated as a snail's shell. Mark a starting line and place the snail's shell 10 metres (33 feet) away from it.

The players will be the snails. They gather at the starting line and wait for the starting signal. Then, they hurry at a snail's pace to the snail shell. The snail to win the medal is the one who needs exactly one minute to cover the distance. The referee monitors the time.

Telling Time — develops time estimating skills. Students may be surprised how difficult it is to estimate time. Use this experience as a discussion starter about having patience with others.

Lemon Hockey

You will need two old umbrellas, lemons, and tape to mark the tracks. Mark out the race tracks with tape. The players use the umbrellas (turned upside down) as hockey sticks, and the lemons as the pucks.

The aim of the game is to push the lemon forward to the end of the track. The catch is that as soon as a player's lemon leaves the track, the player must start all over again. The winners of the heats then play against each other until one person is left.

(**Note:** As an alternative to lemons, you can use balloons filled with water.)

Health — develops ability to deal with frustration when students see that just about everyone is experiencing the same problems.

Gliding

You will need a blanket, paper glider(s), and a large playing area. Mark a starting line and place a blanket approximately 20 metres (65 feet) away from the starting line.

Students take turns at being the "pilot" of the paper glider. The pilot's first throw is made at the starting line. The pilot waits until the plane lands, and then runs to the landing place to throw the glider again. The pilot that reaches the blanket with the least number of throws wins the competition.

History — as part of a history of flight, discuss how short the first airplane flights were.

Tennis

You need a small hillside, a blanket, and one tennis ball for each player. Place the blanket at the bottom of the hill.

The players roll their balls from the top of the hill, trying to get the ball to land on the blanket. If a player's ball does not land on the blanket, the player has to roll down the hill, pick up the ball, run up the hill, and start again. The person who succeeds in placing the ball on the blanket is the winner. If several players' balls land on the blanket, hold a play-off between them until one winner is left.

(**Note:** Players who wear glasses need to be careful. They should take them off, but not put them in their pockets. Assign a special helper for taking care of glasses or other troublesome items.)

Math — sketch the approximate slope of the hill and measure the angle.

Long Throwing

You will need a variety of challenging items for the players to throw. Possible items include cotton balls, used tea bags, a pair of shoes, small paper boxes, water bombs. Mark a starting line.

Players stand at the starting line and throw the objects as far as they can. The referee notes the distances. The player who throws each item the farthest is the winner. There may be a different winner for each item.

Science — discuss why objects that have very little mass are more difficult to throw a long way than items with more mass.

Fourpede

You will need several pairs of shoes. Mark a starting and finish line.

Players who take part in a race of "fourpedes" must first change into a fourpede. To do this, the children put their hands into a pair of shoes. On all fours, they wait at the starting line for the start signal. As soon as the signal is given, the racers run as fast as possible on all fours to win the race, but without losing their shoes.

Science — introduce the study of animals. What animals have four legs? Are there animals with fewer legs? With more legs?

Surfing

You will need a rope, two sturdy mature trees, and a "surfboard" (e.g., a paper or plastic bag, a baking tin, or a skateboard). Tie the rope tightly between two trees at about the average height of the players.

The surfer stands on the surfboard, where the rope is tied to one of the trees. When the starting signal is given, the surfer drags himself along the rope to reach the other tree. The referee notes the time each competitor takes, and the surfer with the best time wins the game.

(**Note:** You can make the game even more challenging by appointing a referee to give points for the surfer who maintains the best posture during the run.)

Science — surfing is a great example of friction. Try all the different objects suggested for surfboards, and predict which ones will move the best, and why.

Basketball

You will need a table, a table tennis ball, nine small cups (paper, plastic, or ceramic mugs), and sand or small stones. The court is a simple table, and the basketball is a table tennis ball. Set up the nine cups in the middle of the table: three rows with three cups each. Put some sand or small stones in the cups to help keep them from falling over.

This type of basketball is a little bit different from the original game, but it is definitely fun! Organize the students into two teams. Team A and team B line up at each side of the table. Draw lots to determine who will start the game. The first team bounces the ball onto the table trying to make it jump into one of the cups. Each hit is worth a point. If the ball misses the cups, the other team takes its turn. After ten rounds, there should be a winning team. If the score is tied, the game continues until one team leads by a point.

(**Note:** This game can be even more fun and challenging if you use several balls at once.)

Language Arts — however fun this game is, it is not the original game of basketball. Have students research the history of basketball.

Table Tennis

You will need a table, five table tennis balls, tape to mark the centre line across a table.

Organize two teams with an equal number of players. Line up the five table tennis balls along the centre line. One team lines up on one side of the table and the other team lines up on the other side. As soon as the starting signal is given, the two teams try to blow the balls across the centre line. The referee watches the game carefully and as soon as all five balls are on the side of the other team, he blows the whistle and gives a point to the winning team. Place the balls back on the centre line, and start the game again. The team leading by two points wins the game.

Science — discuss balanced forces and why it is so difficult to blow the balls across the line.

Team Football

You will need a small ball (e.g., tennis ball).

This game is played in teams with equal numbers of players. The first team removes their shoes and socks and sits in a circle. One of the players takes the small ball between his or her feet. At the starting signal, the ball is immediately passed to the person sitting to the left — but players can use only their feet. If the ball falls to the ground, the team starts over. Players need to move slowly and with concentration. The team is finished when the ball completes the circle. The referee notes the time. Then the next team takes its turn. The team with the best time wins the game.

Language Across the Curriculum — add another dimension to this game. Assign a topic (from any subject) that students are studying. The player with the ball cannot pass it on until he or she has shared a piece of information about the topic. Students may not repeat previously stated information.

Building Towers

You will need a large lawn or grassy area and one hoop per team.

Students work in teams or groups of ten. Each team gets a hoop, which they put on the lawn some distance away from the other teams. Each team is to think about how to place as many children as possible in the middle of the hoop by building a tower. Teams have five minutes to build their tower. An appointed referee evaluates the towers. Each person within the hoop counts as one point, and the referee might give an extra point for special arrangements.

(**Note:** Since the towers usually don't last very long, spectators should watch from a safe distance, and photographers should be ready to take their pictures quickly.)

Dual Combat

You will need blindfolds and small stones, marbles or sugar cubes, and buckets. Mark a starting line and a finish line, and place the buckets at the finish line.

The game is called Dual Combat because two skills (walking and throwing) are combined, and the teams always work in pairs. The teams gather at the starting line. One team member is blindfolded. He or she gets a small stone, marble, or sugar cube and has to bring this item to the bucket at the finish line. The partner's task is to give directions to help the blindfolded person walk to the bucket and drop the item in it. The first team to get the item into the bucket wins.

(**Note:** Instead of blindfolding somebody, try the special glasses used for sleeping on long airplane flights. Ask your friends or relatives if they have such glasses.)

Health — increases sensitivity towards others.

Language Arts — develops communication skills.

Sack Ball

You will need a large empty garbage bag, a chair, and ten small balloons. Mark a starting line and then place a chair about 3 metres (10 feet) away from the line.

Form teams with four to five players. One team member stands on the chair holding a big empty garbage bag in his or her hands. The team members stand at the starting line. They have ten small balloons in their hands. Their task is to throw the balloons to the person standing on the chair. The person on the chair must catch the balloons with the garbage bag. As soon as all the balloons have been thrown, the game is over. The balloons that were caught in the garbage bag are counted. The team with the best score wins the game.

Language Arts — insert a piece of paper with a story-starter in each balloon. After the game have each student take a balloon and write a story to go with the starter.

100-Metre Sprint

You will need skipping ropes and an area where you can set up tracks that are 100 metres (328 feet) long. (**Note:** Depending on the physical condition, age, and so forth of the students, you may want to decrease the distance they must cover.)

Two athletes line up next to each other. They are to cover a distance of 100 metres — not by running, but by skipping together. A little practice might be useful before starting the game. It is more important for the teams to find their rhythm than to be very fast.

Physical Education — emphasize the importance of establishing a rhythm for skipping with a partner. This may mean speeding up or slowing down to accommodate one another. Extend the concept of working together to any other group projects the students may be working on.

Rowing Regatta for Eight

You will need a chair or a tree and a large open distance from the chair or tree. Mark a starting line 50 metres (160 feet) away from the chair or tree.

The teams have nine members. Eight people stand behind one another with their hands on the shoulders of the person standing in front. Their backs are to the tree or chair. The ninth member of the team is the only person who can see the tree or chair.

This person is facing forward and stands in front of the first rower. His or her job is to give orders on how to reach the target as soon as possible. Two or three teams start at the same time and, backwards, row a race.

Social Studies — discuss why there has to be only one person giving orders and relate this discussion to government systems hierarchies.

100-Metre Backward Running

You will need to mark two lines about 100 metres (320 feet) apart.

Students will work in pairs. Their first job is to decide on a whistle they will use in the game. One half of the team lines up facing backwards along one line. Their partners line up directly across from them along the other line, also facing backwards. At the starting signal, the pairs of children run backwards, using their whistling to find each other. Looking around is forbidden! The team that meets first, wins the game.

Music — use this game as a warm-up for music class. After the game have students demonstrate their whistles and learn a song to whistle as a group.

Trotting

You will need a large object to use as a post in the race. Mark a starting line, and place the object a good distance from this point.

The children play in teams of three. The stronger children on the team kneel down close to each other at the starting line. The third child on the team climbs on the backs of the "horses," placing one knee on each horse. The rider should not move too far forward as this hurts and bothers the horses. When all the teams are ready, the starting signal is given, and the horses start running. They must go to the post, around it, and back to the starting line. If the horses somehow lose their rider, the team has to start all over again.

History/Social Science — this game is not easy, and after playing it students studying pioneers may better understand the hardships that settlers faced. Discuss the difficulties that settlers encountered as they opened up new territories across the country.

Monster Volleyball

You will need strips of fabric or lengths of rope, little flags and a rope to mark out the volleyball field, and a balloon to use as the volleyball. The field is half the size of a regular volleyball field. Once the flags are positioned, fix a rope in the middle of the field at a height of approximately 1.5 metres (5 feet).

The children are in teams of three. They line up next to each other and their arms are tied together with the fabric, thus making a "monster." The monster's task is to push the balloon into the other team's half of the field, by using only their "monster" arms. They must not let the balloon touch the ground or the other team scores a point. If the balloon goes out of bounds, it also means a point for the other team. The first team to get five points is the winning team. (**Note:** If a lot of students want to participate, just form larger monsters with four or five members.)

Geography — in this game there are no walls, but the ball can go "out of bounds." Introduce the concept of boundaries. How does a country determine and keep its boundaries?

Social Studies — discuss how the multi-part "monster" in this game is a small system — it has different parts that work together. Use this game to start a discussion about systems in general, or perhaps a specific system, such as local transportation.

Summer Sledding

You will need a starting line, an item to use for a post, and a blanket for each team. Set up a race course with a starting line and a post that each team must go around before returning to the starting line.

The sledding teams have three members. One child sits on the blanket, and the other two members each take hold of one corner of the blanket. The person who is sitting must hold on tight, because when the starting signal goes, the ride will be fast! Two teams can race at one time. A team who loses the person on the blanket has lost the game.

(**Note:** This is an exciting game. Encourage the assigned school reporters and photographers to attend.)

Language Arts — discuss why this game is called "Summer Sledding."

Ambulance Team

Every sports event needs an ambulance service, not only for injured players, but for tired ones as well. This ambulance service is very special, and is more a fun activity than a serious service.

Three children kneel down, close to each other. The "injured" or tired person lies down on the backs of the three children. Slowly, the ambulance moves forward. The faster the ambulance moves, the funnier the activity becomes. You can have a race between different ambulance teams. Five ambulance teams could line up at a starting line and start moving as soon as the signal is given. If the "injured" or tired person falls down, the team has to start all over again.

Health — students who participate in the Ambulance Team may be interested in taking a first aid course.

Horseracing

You will need to mark a starting and finish line 50 metres (160 feet) apart, and each team needs a long stick (e.g., a broom handle).

The children form teams of three, and decide which two will be the horses, and who will be the rider. The rider gets the long stick. The two horses get down on the floor and put their feet up on the stick. The horses race on their arms and hands. It is forbidden during the race for the horses to put their feet on the floor. The teams gather at the starting line, waiting for the signal. (Their position is quite uncomfortable, so they will be champing at the bit to go.) The teams run at a gallop, and the team reaching the finish line first is the winner.

(**Note:** For younger horses, set a shorter course of only 30 metres (100 feet))

Language Arts — teach a lesson on point of view. Have each student write a paragraph about the race, from their point of view — that is, the horse, or the rider. Students can then compare descriptions of the same experience. Be sure to emphasize how they are similar and how they are different.

Relay Race

You will need a marker of some kind (e.g., a chair or a tree) for the course. Set up the marker and starting line approximately 50 metres (160 feet) apart.

Arrange the children into two to five teams of six to eight members. (Teams should have an equal number of players.) Each team member is assigned a number from one to eight (depending on the number of players per team). Each child must remember his or her number. The teams line up at the starting line and the game starts when the referee calls a number. All the children with this number run to the marker, and back to the group. The team whose runner is fastest gets a point. After 20 turns, the game is over. The team with the highest number of points wins the game.

Math — instead of calling out a number, call out a division question. If the answer corresponds to the student's number, he or she must run to the marker and back.

Balloon Relay Race

You will need a marker (e.g., chair, tree, lantern), one plate, and one inflated balloon per team.

Two teams of runners line up at the starting line. The first

Cooperative Learning — teaches valuable "learning to learn skills" such as the easy way is not always available and take your time to complete a task properly.

runner gets a plate with a balloon lying on top. As soon as the starting signal is given, the player runs to the marker and back to the starting line. There, the plate is passed to the next runner. However, runners are forbidden to hold the balloon with their hands or head. If the balloon falls to the ground, the team has to start again. (The players will learn quickly that they need a lot of time to make it around the course.)

Wooden Relay Race

You will need a marker and a starting line, as well as an object for players to carry as the relay.

Form teams with the same number of children. The first person to go gets the relay object, and has to put it between his or her feet. The racers can either jump or crawl to a marked point and then back to the starting line, where the racer passes the relay to the next person, who immediately starts his race. The team who finishes first, wins the game.

Creative Thinking — encourages decision-making skills. The students are limited as to how they can carry the relay. They must decide quickly which method they will use, and act on it.

Marathon

You will need a stick decorated with balloons set about 15–20 metres (50-65 feet) away from a starting line.

The runners line up next to each other at the starting line. The first runner starts the race by running out to the decorated stick and back to the starting line. The runner then politely shakes hands with someone else on the team. They link arms and then run the course together, shaking hands and linking arms with someone else, when they return to the starting line. Then the three of them run the course. This goes on until all the members of the team are running in a line. They should try not to break the chain. When all runners have done the course, the team will have covered the marathon distance.

There are no medals for winning in this activity, but the runners will probably get lots of cheering and applause!

Math — practise multiple-digit addition by adding the distance run each time. Calculate the distance the first runner must run!

68

Pair Skating

You will need a marker (e.g., chair or object) placed about 20 metres (65 feet) from the starting line.

This game requires four equal teams to line up at the starting line. The first person asks a second one to run with him or her, takes the second person's arm, and the two run to the marker. The first person stays there, and the second person runs back to fetch the third person. The third person runs back, and so on, until one team has gathered all its members at the marker. The first team to do so wins the race.

Math — present the game as a math problem. If the distance between the marker and the starting line is 20 metres (65 feet), how many metres does each runner run? How many metres in total does the team run?

69

Walking Race

You will need to make two large cards marked "A" and "B," and flags or chalk to mark out the teams' "home" areas.

The rules for this game are very strict: Players must walk, not run. Anyone who runs is excluded.

Form two teams, A and B. They line up, face-to-face along a centre line with about an arms length between them. Each team has a "home" 20 metres (65 feet) away, where they are safe during the game. "Home" is 2 metres in diameter (7 feet) and can be marked with chalk or small flags.

Play begins when the referee holds up one of the two large cards. If card A is raised, the members of team A have to catch the members of team B. The team B players start heading for their "home" immediately. Any members of team B who are caught before reaching "home," drop out of the game. Then the referee holds up the other card, and so on. The team with only three members left loses the game.

Critical Thinking — discuss what will happen if the "home" circles are made smaller.

Pentathlon

You will need big garbage bags and string. Mark a starting line and a finish line for the teams.

The children form teams of five players. Each player climbs into a garbage bag and uses string as a belt to keep the garbage bag up. Standing side by side, each player joins hands with the others on the team. Then there are two possible ways to play:

1. Teams wait at the starting line for the signal. Each pentathlon team jumps one after another to the finish line. Times are recorded, and the team with the fastest time wins the game.

2. All pentathlon teams gather at the starting line. When the signal is given, they jump the distance to the finish line. The team that reaches the finish line first wins the game.

Language Arts — create a special vocabulary book. Include the meaning and background of the word "pentathlon." Also include words related to the other games and activities.

Long Jump

You will need a tape measure. Mark a starting line with tape or chalk.

The players form teams with equal numbers of members. The first person on team A jumps from the starting line as far as possible. The second player starts where the first jumper stopped.

And so on, until the last member of team A has jumped. The referee measures the whole distance from the first jump to the last jump. Then the next team follows the same procedure. The team with the longest distance wins the medal.

Math — instead of adding all the distances for one team, ask students to multiply them.

Remote Control Soccer

You will need a soccer ball. Mark two ends for the goal keepers.

Each team elects a team leader who will control his team from a remote place. The rest of the players take the field. When the starting signal is given, the only players who are allowed to run are those whose names are called out by the team leader. The other players are not allowed to move (except for the goal keepers, who can move as often as they like, but must stay close to the goal.) The team leader must decide very quickly who should go on playing the ball.

You can vary the game by having teachers playing against pupils, or by playing with a tennis ball or a balloon filled with water instead of a regular soccer ball.

Communication — teams work out a silent signal system and use this system to play again. Compare which game was more successful and why.

Slow Race

You will need to mark a starting and a finish line.

The cyclists wait at the starting line. All cyclists should start at the same time. You can help by making sure everyone is seated on their bicycles before the start signal. Let the cyclists get on their bikes, and then a helper can hold them in place. When the start signal is given, the helpers move off as quickly as possible, and the cyclists start riding their bikes — but as slowly as possible. The person who reaches the finish line last is the winner.

Language Arts — read the story The Tortoise and the Hare and discuss how this game is like the story.

Bicycle Slalom

You will need bags, clothing, and other easily seen objects. Prepare a slalom track by putting a variety of these objects on the track. Have the cyclists do a test ride to make sure that the objects have been positioned correctly.

Each cyclist has to ride the slalom course as quickly as possible. The time for everyone's run is recorded. The three cyclists with the fastest time are honored with medals.

Math — graph the positions of the objects on the obstacle course. To mark the axes at 0,0, the students should stand on the south side and plot the course from west to east.

Pushing Bicycles

You will need blindfolds for the cyclists. Use a piece of chalk to draw a circle with a 2-metre (7 feet) diameter on the ground. Blindfold the cyclists.

The cyclists form a line 30–50 metres (100-160 feet) away from the circle. One by one, they push their bikes towards the circle. When the player thinks that he or she has reached the middle of the circle, he or she gives a sign. The referee marks the final position for each player. (If possible, have the referee use a different color of chalk for each player.) When all cyclists have pushed their bicycles, the winner is the person who made it closest to the circle.

This is a good activity for learning to estimate distances based on the approximate size of one's stride. This is a skill that is useful in science, geography, and math.

The Tricky Eight

You will need paint or lots of colored chalk, and four sets of cards numbered 1–6. Paint (or use chalk to draw) a large figure "8" on the floor of the playground or other asphalt surface at the school.

Four referees are assigned to watch the cyclists. The participants ride their bikes around the figure "8" in an elegant and skilful way. Each referee evaluates the ride, and lifts up the cards with numbers from 1–6 to show the score. A rider's score is determined by adding the points from all the referees and calculating the average. The winners have the highest scores.

Language Arts — ask students to write a description of their performance.

Recognizing Your Bicycle

You will need ten to twenty bicycles and three blindfolds.

All the bicycles are placed next to each other. Three bike owners are blindfolded. Move some of the bicycles to different positions once the players have their blindfolds on. The players must now find their own bike, but only by touching the bikes. The person who finds his or her bike first is the winner.

Science — students who excel at this activity are likely keen observers. Observation is a skill that is especially useful for science. Introduce the term "properties" and discuss qualitative and quantitative observations.

Snowman Relay

You will need to build a snowman before the game starts. Use a real hat or a bucket for his hat, and a carrot for his nose. All participants should be involved in making the snowman. Mark a starting line a few metres away from the snowman.

Two groups with the same number of players gather at the starting line. The first member of team A throws a snowball and tries to make the snowman's hat fall off. If the hat falls down, the team receives a point. After all the team members have tried to hit the hat, the team with the highest score wins the game. If nobody succeeds in hitting the hat, the game continues with children throwing alternately until, finally, the hat falls down.

Cooperative Learning — older students are likely to help younger students push and lift the larger snowballs that make up the snowman. This can be a good way to let older and younger students find reading or math buddies — or just a friend.

Bobsleigh

You will need plastic bags or trays. Mark a starting line and a finish line in the snow.

The bobsleigh racers use a plastic bag or plastic tray as their sled. All the bobsleigh racers sit next to each other on their sleds at the starting line. The racers can use only their hands and feet for pushing forward. The crowd should wait at the end of the course for the racers to come. The fastest racer wins the game.

Science — investigate different kinds of plastic bags and hard plastics to find out which one is the fastest. Students should remember to think about other factors that could affect the speed of the racers (e.g., Are all the tests done on the same day? Is each bobsleigh the same size? Do you have the same people riding the bobsleigh?)

Caterpillar Roll

You will need to make sure that children are dressed properly for outdoor winter play. Mark a finish line at the bottom of a gently sloping hill.

The warmly dressed children can do a caterpillar roll by laying down at the top of the hill, and rolling down horizontally to the bottom. The roller who crosses the finish line first is the winner.

Children might not be participating in every outdoor winter activity. Keep them active with other ideas, such as the following:

- stamping patterns into the snow
- building a snow sculpture (e.g., the *Everybody Wins* mascot)
- using water color to paint or splash pictures in the snow

These activities are just for fun and for socializing.

The Ring

You will need an inflated swimming ring or inner tube. Place the ring on the ground and mark a line about 10–20 metres (35-65 feet) from the ring.

The players stand on this line and try to throw snowballs into the middle of the ring. Each player gets three snowballs. The players who hit the middle of the ring the most are the winners.

Physical Education — refines hand-eye coordination.

Water Ball

You will need buckets, a small children's wading pool, and forty table tennis balls. Fill the pool with water and add the balls. Before the game starts, the referee makes sure that the water is stirred up and has lots of bubbles.

Two teams with three members each are positioned around the pool. Each child gets a drinking straw. The aim of the game is to transport the table tennis balls from the water to the bucket using only the straw. When there are no table tennis balls left in the pool, the teams count the number of balls in their bucket. The scores are recorded, then other pairs of teams play. At the end of the game, the team with the highest score wins.

Science — investigate the effects of pressure, which allowed the students to lift the table tennis balls with a straw.

Water Race

You will need a shallow pool, such as a pool for non-swimmers. Tell students that all races are strenuous. But a running race in water is really challenging — and also a lot of fun!

Depending on the size of the pool you have access to, there could be from three to ten children racing at the same time. The children line up at one end and run in the water to the other end. The fastest runners qualify for the next heat. The race goes on until everybody has had a turn, and only three winners are left.

Science — ask students what they think running in vegetable oil would be like. How about in molasses? Discuss how these substances are alike and different.

Water Football

You will need an old plastic football, colored headbands or bathing caps, and a shallow pool for non-swimmers.

To play this football match, take the old plastic football, cut a hole in it, and sink it to the bottom of the pool. Using the waterlogged ball play a regular football game. Teams can be distinguished by their different headbands or bathing caps. A goal is scored when the ball touches the side walls of the pool.

Science — investigate the properties that make objects float and sink.

Sailing

You will need paper, colored flags or sticks, and a small wading pool.

Each player is the captain of his or her own boat. Each captain makes a paper sailing boat by folding a piece of paper according to the following instructions.

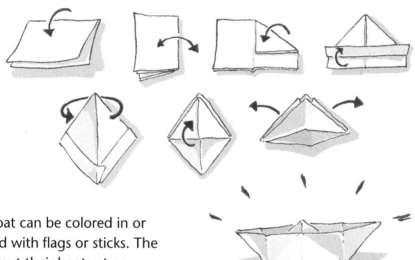

The boat can be colored in or decorated with flags or sticks. The captains put their boats at one end of the pool. When the starting signal is given, the captains start to blow their boats to the other end of the pool. Instead of blowing, captains can use a paper fan to move their boats.

Art — the paper boat in this activity is an example of the Japanese paper-folding art called origami. Find some books with instructions for other origami figures for students to make in art class. (**Note:** Most origami is made from perfectly square pieces of paper. Precisely cut square origami paper is often available at art stores or some toy stores.)

Water Tennis

You will need paper or plastic cups, table tennis balls, a table, and water.

Each player gets a cup that is three-quarters filled with water. The cup also has a table tennis ball, which floats on the surface of the water. The cups are placed on a table in front of the players. The challenge is to blow the table tennis ball out of the cup.

Partner Swimming

You will need access to a large swimming pool for this activity.

Two people swim next to each other holding the other's hand. The person who swims on the left side paddles with their left hand, and the person on the right, with their right hand. Use the length of the pool for the race. Five pairs of swimmers race against each other. The best teams compete until the three fastest pairs of swimmers are left.

Physical Education — use this game as a warm-up or warm-down in school swimming lessons. Discuss water safety rules and practices when you use this exercise.

The Noise Game

You will need a metal baking tray and about twenty small objects. Choose objects that make a strange noise when they are dropped onto the tray (e.g., a box of matches, a book, a pin, keys, coins, a pen).

Before the game starts, the players carefully observe the objects and listen to the sounds the objects make when they are dropped on the tray. To play, students keep their backs turned, and the referee throws the objects one by one onto the tray. The players try to guess what each object is. Each correct answer counts for one point, and the person with the highest score wins the game.

Learning Skills — adapt this game to help students improve their memory skills. Instead of hearing the objects drop again, have students recall the objects from memory. Help students learn to use this skill to remember special vocabulary, place names on maps, information in charts, and so forth.

The Mysterious Word

You will need paper or a blackboard.

The children form groups of four. The game leader thinks of a word and draws a box for each letter of the word. For example, COMPUTER.

Taking turns, each team may choose one letter. If the letter is part of the word, it is written in the appropriate box(es).

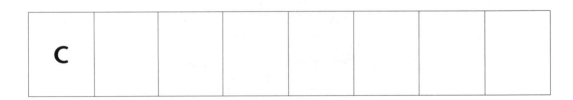

Teams take turns until one team is sure they know the word. The team says it out loud, and if the word is correct, they score points equal to the number of boxes that have *not* been filled in so far. For the example above, the number of points would be seven. If the word is not correct, the guessing team is excluded for one turn. You may want to set a score limit (e.g., 20 points), and the team who achieves that number of points wins the game.

Math — use numbers instead of letters. Choose a final value for the last box and then fill in a few of the other boxes with numbers. Students guess what numbers and symbols go in the other boxes to make a balanced equation.

Quiz Pantomime

You will need a blackboard or an easel with paper, a stop watch for timing the game, plus chalk or felt-tipped markers.

The children are arranged in teams with five to ten members. Team A starts, and chooses one team member to stand with his or her back to the blackboard. The game leader then writes or draws a word or object on the board (e.g., "ball"). Team A uses gestures to help the other team member guess the object — no words are allowed. They have 20 seconds. If the player guesses the word, the team gets a point. There are five turns for each team, and the team with the highest score wins the game. If the score is even, the teams go on until one team wins the game.

Social Studies — useful activity for reviewing historical events.

The Present

You will need a space that provides a clear view to all players.

Players are arranged in teams. One player sits down in front of the audience (the other team members), and pretends to open a present. What could be in the present? It could be anything: a balloon, a snail, an elephant, or a bucket with strawberries...The player is only allowed to use gestures, and the teams must interpret those gestures to guess the contents of the present. For each correct answer, a team gets one point. The first team to six points wins.

(**Note:** To prevent too many words being called out at any time, the teams could agree that a person who guesses incorrectly is excluded from the game for one turn.)

Language Arts — play the activity to review spelling words or to re-enact part of a reading assignment.

Picture Riddle

You will need paper and pencils or pens.

The participants of the game are divided into teams of equal number. Each team chooses two people to play. The game leader thinks of an object, and tells one player in each team what that object is. The other player from each team sits at a table with a piece of paper and a pen. The player stands behind his or her partner and uses their fingers to draw a picture of the object on the player's back. The player sitting at the table draw the lines that are being drawn on their back. As soon as a sitting player believes that he or she can identify the object, they may call the word out loud. If the answer is correct, the turn is over, and the team gets a point. If the answer is wrong, the team is excluded from the game for one turn.

Art — refines sketching abilities.

Book Balance

You will need books and elastic bands. (**Note:** To give all players an equal chance, the books should be similar in size and weight.)

A book that is held closed with an elastic band is set upright on each player's palm. The players must balance it for as long as possible, while the audience counts off the seconds out loud. Each participant may try three times to set a new record.

Science — investigate how the size and mass of the book affects the average length of time that students can hold the book. You should have several different books to test.

The Letter Snail

You will need paper and pens or pencils.

Each player writes all the letters of the alphabet on a piece of paper. Then they think of a word that consists of as many different letters as possible (e.g., xylophone). Players can cross out each letter that is used in their word. Participants keep playing until they have crossed out all the letters. The person who needed the fewest words is the winner.

Language Across the Curriculum — use terminology from any subject. Try restricting players to using only words related to a specific topic of study in math, social studies, language arts, or science.

Ring Gymnastics

You may need a 30-cm ruler or a 30-cm piece of rope for each participant.

Participants bend forward and form a ring with their arms. They must step through this ring without "breaking" it (i.e., they must hold onto their hands). If the players can achieve this goal, the activity can then be done backwards. The three fastest gymnasts win the game.

(**Note:** This exercise is easier when the athletes have an object, such as a ruler or a piece of rope, to increase the size of the ring.)

Physical Education — use this activity as an introduction to gymnastics and working on the mats.

Balloon Competition

You will need two balloons and a wool sweater, jacket, or blanket.

Form two teams and give each team an inflated balloon. The teams take their balloon and rub it on a wool sweater, jacket, or blanket. The teams then push their balloon toward the ceiling of the room, where it will stick for a while. While the balloons stay there, the children can play other games. After a while, the balloons will come down. The team whose balloon stays up for the longest time, wins.

Science — introduce students to static electricity — the reason the balloons stick to the ceiling.

Long Breath

You do not need any materials or equipment.

All participants take a deep breath and then hum a soft tone. People who run out of breath drop out of the game. The person who hums the tone for the longest time is the winner.

Science — this is an excellent way to introduce the human respiratory system. Students can come up with their own questions to investigate, based on what happened during this activity (e.g., why some people ran out of breath quickly, and others seemed to go on for a long time).